WONDER WOMAN MYTHOLOGY

Wonder Woman and the Villains of Myth

by STEVE KORTÉ

Wonder Woman created by William Moulton Marston

Consultant:
Laurel Bowman
Department of Greek and Roman Studies
University of Victoria
British Columbia, Canada

CAPSTONE PRESS
a capstone imprint

Published by Capstone Press in 2017
1710 Roe Crest Drive
North Mankato, Minnesota 56003
www.mycapstone.com

STAR37673

Library of Congress Cataloging-in-Publication Data is available on
the Library of Congress website.

ISBN: 978-1-5157-4584-6 (library binding)
ISBN: 978-1-5157-4597-6 (eBook PDF)

Summary: Introduces a variety of villains from Greek, Roman,
Norse, and other world mythologies, and explores how they are
woven into the fabric of Wonder Woman's backstory.

Editor: Christopher Harbo

Designer: Tracy McCabe

Creative Director: Bob Lentz

Production Specialist: Katy LaVigne

Image Credits:
Capstone: Dan Schoening, 17 (inset), Luciano Vecchio, 7,
Rich Pellegrind, 13, Scott Altman, 11, 15, 19, 21, 22, 25, 27;
iStockphoto: Kartmaral, cover (bottom right), Paolo Gaetano
Rocco, 6; Shutterstock: Adwo, 13 (inset), HP Productions, 9 (inset),
tan_tan, 17, Vuk Kostic, cover (left and right), 29; Warner Brothers,
throughout (Wonder Woman and backgrounds)

Printed and bound in the USA.
010061S17

TABLE OF CONTENTS

INTRODUCTION

A Victor Over Villains

Myths are amazing stories of gods, goddesses, heroes, and fantastic creatures. The myths of ancient Greece told classic tales of a race of warrior women known as the Amazons. In more recent stories in comic books, these Amazons lived peacefully together on a hidden island. Then they learned that Ares, the god of war, was plotting to destroy all of humankind. The Amazons held a contest to choose one champion to fight Ares. The winner of that competition was Princess Diana, who became the super hero Wonder Woman.

Princess Diana left the world of the Amazons and traveled to our world to fight Ares. Since then, many amazing stories have been told of her battles against monsters, **mortals**, gods, and demons. Over the years, Wonder Woman has faced evil in all its forms. But perhaps most remarkably of all, many of her villains actually come from classic mythological tales. Come along as Wonder Woman confronts some of the most dangerous villains in myths from around the world.

mortal—human, referring to a being who will eventually die

CHAPTER 1

Evil Gods

ARES

Few gods in Greek mythology were as destructive as Ares, the god of war. Ares was an angry and scheming god. He had many powers, including **immortality** and the ability to change his appearance. He loved war and conflict, and was known as the god of battle frenzy, instead of strategy. No matter what, Ares always encouraged violence to resolve conflicts. His main goal was to see all of the humans on Earth plunged into warfare. He fought against the Greeks during the Trojan War, and delighted in the destruction on that battlefield for 10 long years.

In Wonder Woman **lore**, the Amazons learned that Ares was plotting to destroy all of humankind with a nuclear war. They sent Princess Diana to America to fight him. She trapped Ares within her Golden Lasso of Truth. It forced him to realize that his powers would actually decrease if he killed every human. Without human anger to help him grow stronger, Ares would grow weak and disappear. The war god was furious to be defeated by Wonder Woman. He vowed revenge against her and all of the Amazons.

FACT
Ares was known as Mars in Roman mythology.

UNLUCKY WAR GOD

Ares isn't the only war god in world mythology. Tyr was a noble god of war in Norse mythology. Although he liked bloodshed, he also represented order and justice. But Tyr had very bad luck with animals. A wolf bit off his right hand. Years later, Tyr died in the jaws of a giant dog.

immortality—the ability to live forever

lore—stories passed down over generations

TRITON

Triton was the son of Poseidon, the Greek god of the sea. Triton lived with his father in a golden palace at the bottom of the ocean. He was a strong young man with a human upper body and a scaly fish tail. Although his father was a mighty god, Triton did not always behave **honorably**. Sometimes, he attacked ships and robbed them of their treasures. Triton's most prized possession was a giant horn that was made out of a conch shell. He blew on his horn to announce the arrival of his father. The horn also had the power to cause fear in mortals and gods. One time, Triton fought and defeated a sailor who dared to challenge him in a horn-blowing contest. Triton then drowned his opponent!

Triton first met Wonder Woman when she was swimming in the waters that surrounded Themyscira, the island home of the Amazons. Triton tried to convince her to come live with him. He was interrupted by the arrival of young Prince Arthur from the underwater city of Atlantis. Arthur convinced Diana that Triton did not really love her, and he defeated Triton in a battle. After that, Triton plotted to **humiliate** Wonder Woman. He also vowed revenge on Prince Arthur, who would grow up to become the aquatic super hero Aquaman.

honorable—good and deserving of praise
humiliate—to make someone look or feel foolish or embarrassed

FACT

The world's largest conch shells are known as Triton's trumpets. They can grow up to 20 inches (51 centimeters) long.

AHRIMAN

The world's first **civilizations** and cities appeared in the Near East more than 5,000 years ago. Myths played an important role in those early cultures. In the land of Persia, which is now Iran, Ahriman was the god of darkness and the leader of an army of demons. He was the evil twin of Ahura Mazda, who was the god of light and wisdom. While the twins were still in the **womb**, Ahriman heard his father say, "The firstborn will be king." Ahriman then ripped his way free and tumbled into the world ahead of Ahura Mazda. After that, the twins were forever locked in a power struggle, symbolizing the conflict between good and evil.

In the legend of Wonder Woman, Ahriman killed his twin brother. Ahriman removed Ahura Mazda's heart and magically changed it into gold. Ahriman then moved to the United States and disguised himself as a gambler in the casinos of Las Vegas. Many years later, Wonder Woman discovered his secret identity. She forced him to bring Ahura Mazda back to life.

FACT

In Persian myth, the first man was named Gayomart. Ahura Mazda created him, and Ahriman killed him.

civilization—an organized and advanced society

womb—the hollow organ in female mammals that
holds and nourishes a growing fetus, or baby

CRONUS

The Greek god Cronus had a long history of family problems. First, he forced his cruel father, Uranus — who had been the ruler of the universe — from the throne. Then a **prophet** told Cronus that his own children would overthrow him. As a result, Cronus swallowed his first five children whole when they were born. But his wife tricked him with the sixth. She gave Cronus a rock wrapped in a blanket instead.

That sixth child was Zeus. When he grew up, he forced Cronus to vomit up his brothers and sisters. With their help — and the aid of giants, lightning bolts, and an invisibility helmet — Zeus defeated his father. Cronus was **banished** to Tartarus, which was the lowest level of the underworld known as Hades.

Princess Diana was born when her mother sculpted a child out of clay on Themyscira. The gods on Mount Olympus then brought that sculpture to life. Years later, Cronus was freed from the pits of Tartarus. He vowed revenge on the gods and the peace-loving Amazons. Cronus created his own daughter, Devastation, out of the same clay that formed Diana. Eventually, Devastation teamed up with her father to storm Mount Olympus and battle the gods. Wonder Woman defeated them and shattered the sharp blade that Cronus was carrying. It was the same blade that he had used to defeat his father, Uranus.

prophet—a messenger of God, or a person who tells the future

banished—sent away forever

HEAVY LOAD

The warrior Atlas made the mistake of leading the army of Cronus in the war against Zeus. After Zeus won the war, he made Atlas forever carry the enormous weight of the world and sky on his shoulders.

DEIMOS AND PHOBOS

The war god Ares caused destruction throughout the world. Two of his most eager assistants were his sons, Deimos and Phobos. Deimos was the god of dread and terror. Phobos was the god of fear and panic. Whenever Ares traveled to a battlefield where mortal men were engaged in a war, Deimos and Phobos would join their father. Together, they would whip up a storm of fury that would make the men even more savage.

One of Wonder Woman's most unusual partnerships occurred when she teamed up with Batman. It happened when Deimos and Phobos arrived in Gotham City, along with their sister, Eris, who was the goddess of **strife**. The three siblings took control of the bodies of the Scarecrow, the Joker, and Poison Ivy — some of the Dark Knight's worst enemies. Even worse, Phobos took control of Batman's mind. Wonder Woman helped Batman drive out the evil spirit of Phobos. Together, they defeated Ares' children.

Years later, Wonder Woman became trapped within the snake-filled beard of the Deimos of her world. As the snakes tried to poison her with panic-inducing venom, she threw her razor-sharp tiara at Deimos and defeated him.

strife—a fight or a struggle

DEIMOS

PHOBOS

FACT
A phobia is a type of fear that can sometimes be overwhelming. The word "phobia" comes from Phobos, who caused terror wherever he went.

CHAPTER 2
Angry Goddesses

SEKHMET

Sekhmet was the fierce Egyptian goddess of war. She had the head of a lion and the body of a woman, and she often carried a fire-breathing cobra. Her name meant "the powerful one," and she was a ruthless warrior. Some said that Sekhmet was the daughter of the sun god Ra. Others claimed that she was merely Ra's most trusted soldier.

Sekhmet was widely feared on the battlefield. Eventually, she became so powerful that Ra grew worried that she would destroy all of humankind. Ra arranged for 7,000 jugs of red liquid to be poured onto the ground. Sekhmet lapped it up, thinking it was human blood. She then fell into a deep sleep, which saved the human race from destruction.

Centuries ago, the Amazons of Wonder Woman's world broke into two **tribes**. Hippolyta, the mother of Princess Diana, led one tribe. An Amazon named Antiope led the other tribe, which was called the Bana-Mighdall. They lived in Egypt and worshipped Egyptian gods, including Sekhmet.

When an alien known as Imperiex threatened to destroy the entire galaxy, Sekhmet joined his army and grew even more powerful. Wonder Woman teamed up with Superman and other heroes to defeat Imperiex and his army.

tribe—a group of people who share the same language and way of life

FACT
Ancient Egyptians worshipped Sekhmet
and carved statues of her in black volcanic rock.

A FELINE FELON

One of Wonder Woman's most savage opponents is the
Cheetah, a human-sized cat. Archaeologist Barbara
Minerva ate a poisonous plant and changed into the
Cheetah. She grew razor-sharp claws, sported a
cat-like tail, and gained the strength of a giant cat.

HECATE

Some say that the Greek goddess Hecate was not always evil. When she was younger, she became a trusted **ally** of Zeus and helped him to rule the land, sky, and sea. Hecate could be kind and generous, giving many gifts to mortals. Those gifts included wealth, athletic skills, and victories in wars. As the goddess of **prosperity**, she granted healthy livestock to farmers and unlimited catches to fishermen.

In time, though, Hecate's personality changed, and mortals began to fear her. Hecate practiced dark magic and developed an interest in death. She made many journeys to the underworld of dead souls. Eventually, Hecate became known as the goddess of witchcraft. It was rumored that she danced in the underworld with a pack of howling ghosts. Sometimes, her dance spilled into the world of mortals, where she was accompanied by a pack of howling dogs.

In Wonder Woman's world, Hecate married the Greek god Hades and lived with him in his underworld of dead souls. Hades grew tired of her, though, and took a new wife. This so enraged Hecate that she traveled to Earth and took control of the sorceress Circe. Hecate granted immortality to Circe and gave her magical powers. In return, Circe launched a giant battle known as the War of the Gods in an attempt to destroy the gods of Mount Olympus. It took all of the powers of Wonder Woman and the heroes of Earth to win the war.

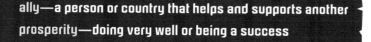

ally—a person or country that helps and supports another
prosperity—doing very well or being a success

HAUNTED HOUNDS

Even in modern-day Greece, some people believe Hecate still haunts graveyards. She is said to walk with a pack of black dogs at her side and search for souls to take to the underworld.

THE FURIES

The Furies were three goddesses of **vengeance** in Greek mythology. They were born when Cronus killed the sky god Uranus with a sharp blade. Uranus bled onto the earth, and the Furies rose from three drops of his blood. Their names were Tisiphone, Megaera, and Alecto. The Furies had snakes for hair and giant bat wings on their backs. They usually lived in the lowest part of the underworld and tormented wicked souls. The Furies also enjoyed traveling to the world of mortals to torture people who had shed blood within their families.

In the mythology of Wonder Woman, the Furies had the power to change their looks. They often took the form of three mortals — a young girl, a middle-aged mother, and an aged grandmother.

When Nazi Germany invaded Greece during World War II (1939–1945), Tisiphone gave some of her magical powers to a young Greek woman named Helena Kosmatos. Calling herself Fury, Helena became a savage opponent of the Nazis and fought alongside Wonder Woman.

vengeance—action that you take to pay someone back for harm done to you or someone you care about

CHAPTER 3
Menacing Magicians

CIRCE

In Greek mythology, Circe was a moon-worshipping witch who lived in a mighty palace on her own island. She used her magical powers for evil, and she especially loved to change visitors to her island into animals. When the mighty warrior Odysseus docked his boat in the harbor of Circe's island, she invited his crew to dine with her. She then changed all of the sailors into pigs! Odysseus talked Circe into undoing the spell, and he then spent the next several years with her. During that time, they had three sons. One of the sons would later kill Odysseus.

In the tales of Wonder Woman, Circe plotted against the Amazons for centuries. Circe's almost unlimited magical powers made her a dangerous enemy.

The sorceress once brought the mythical monster Medusa back to life. This horrible creature had snakes for hair. Circe also put a magical spell on Wonder Woman that temporarily turned her into a mortal. Even without her powers, Wonder Woman continued her fight for justice.

Years later, Circe changed the entire male population of New York City into animals known as Bestiamorphs. Because women were not affected by the spell, Wonder Woman joined forces with Earth's greatest female super heroes. They defeated the sorceress and broke Circe's spell.

MAKING A MONSTER

Circe could rarely be trusted. The sea god Glaucus fell in love with a beautiful sea spirit named Scylla. Glaucus asked Circe for a love potion, but Circe was in love with Glaucus herself. The jealous sorceress made a concoction that turned Scylla into a hideous monster.

MORGAINE LE FAY

In Celtic myths from thousands of years ago, Morgaine le Fay was a beautiful and powerful sorceress. Some stories say she learned magic while living in a **nunnery**. Others tell that the legendary wizard Merlin taught her to cast spells. Either way, she could also fly and was able to change her appearance at will.

In addition to her skills as a sorceress, Morgaine was the half-sister of King Arthur. He was the mighty ruler of the kingdom of Camelot. Yet the two half-siblings had a difficult relationship. Morgaine often plotted against Arthur. She tried to steal his sword, Excalibur, and did anything she could to bring him pain.

In Wonder Woman lore, Morgaine le Fey grew obsessed with holding on to her youthful beauty. She ordered the creature known as Etrigan the Demon to kidnap Wonder Woman. The ancient sorceress wanted to live forever, so she cast a spell to steal the Amazing Amazon's immortal powers. Her scheme backfired on her, though, because at that time Wonder Woman had temporarily become a mortal. The spell instantly aged Morgaine le Fey, and she crumbled into dust.

FACT

Long ago, a **mirage** seen on the ocean was called a fata morgana. Sailors believed that Morgaine le Fay had created it with her sorcery.

nunnery—a religious community in which a nun lives and works

mirage—something that appears to be there but is not; mirages are caused by light rays bending where air layers of different temperatures meet

CHAPTER 4
Kings and Tricksters

IXION

Ixion was a wicked Greek king who fell in love with a young girl named Dia. In order to marry Dia, he agreed to pay a fortune to her father, who was an old man named Eioneus. Ixion invited Eioneus to attend the wedding, but Ixion had no intention of paying the fee. Instead, he set a trap near the entrance to the palace. Eioneus tumbled into a fire pit and burned to death. Ixion became the first mortal man in history to kill one of his own relatives!

Ixion became an outcast after this, but the Greek god Zeus eventually forgave Ixion. He invited Ixion to dine with the gods on Mount Olympus. Ixion promptly fell in love with Hera, the wife of Zeus, and tried to steal her away. This so enraged Zeus that the angry god chained Ixion to a revolving wheel of fire. Ixion was forever trapped on the flaming wheel as it soared through the nighttime sky.

It was several centuries later when Wonder Woman
encountered Ixion. Phobos, the god of fear, freed
Ixion from his wheel of fire and then commanded
Ixion to attack Boston. Ixion destroyed much of
Boston's harbor area and killed hundreds of innocent
people. Wonder Woman captured Ixion, but he refused to
be returned to his immortal wheel of torture. He died in a
confrontation with a squadron of fighter pilots.

LOKI

Loki was a mischief-making trickster god in Norse mythology. He loved to deceive others to get what he wanted. Loki was also a magician and a shape-shifter, able to take on the appearance of anything he chose. The gods tolerated Loki until he caused the death of Balder, the god of light. Loki was imprisoned in a cave deep below the earth and chained to a rock. To punish him even more, a giant serpent crawled on top of Loki and dripped boiling hot blood laced with **venom** onto his face. Loki's painful thrashing caused earthquakes.

Wonder Woman first met Loki when the trickster god was living in the all-male city of Elam. The men of Elam proposed a competition against the women from the nearby city of Noman. If the women lost the contest, they would become slaves to the men of Elam. Loki brought in mighty warriors from the past, including Paul Bunyan and the Black Knight, to make sure that the women would lose. The ruler of Noman asked for Wonder Woman's help, and Diana agreed to join the competition. After Wonder Woman defeated Loki's warriors, the trickster god disappeared.

AWFUL OFFSPRING

Loki was the father of several terrifying children. One was a giant savage wolf known as Fenrir. Even the Norse gods were afraid of Fenrir. They tried to trick the wolf into putting his head through a collar made of heavy chains, but Fenrir merely had to stretch his neck to break the chains. Loki also had a frightful daughter named Hel. As the goddess of death, Hel was half-human and half-rotting flesh. She ruled the kingdom of dead souls in her ice-cold palace.

CONCLUSION

Wonder Woman left her home with a mission to defeat one of the most notorious villains of Greek mythology. Since then, she has chosen to remain in our world and has bravely fought hundreds of other evildoers. Many of these dangerous villains come from mythological tales that have been told for centuries. In the myths of Wonder Woman, one fact is certain. When dangerous villains threaten the innocent, Wonder Woman will stand strong to protect us all.

venom—a poisonous liquid produced by some animals

GLOSSARY

ally (AL-eye)—a person or country that helps and supports another

banished (BAN-isht)—sent away forever

civilization (si-vuh-ly-ZAY-shuhn)—an organized and advanced society

honorable (ON-ur-uh-buhl)—good and deserving of praise

humiliate (hyoo-MIL-ee-ate)—to make someone look or feel foolish or embarrassed

immortality (i-mor-TAL-uh-tee)—the ability to live forever

lore (LORE)—a collection of knowledge and traditions of a particular group that has been passed down over generations

mirage (muh-RAZH)—something that appears to be there but is not; mirages are caused by light rays bending where air layers of different temperatures meet

mortal (MOR-tuhl)—human, referring to a being who will eventually die

nunnery (NUHN-ur-ee)—a religious community in which a nun lives and works

prophet (PROF-it)—a messenger of God, or a person who tells the future

prosperity (prahs-PAYR-uh-tee)—doing very well or being a success

strife (STRIFE)—a fight or a struggle

tribe (TRIBE)—a group of people who share the same language and way of life

vengeance (VEN-juhnss)—action that you take to pay someone back for harm done to you or someone you care about

venom (VEN-uhm)—a poisonous liquid produced by some animals

womb (WOOM)—the hollow organ in female mammals that holds and nourishes a growing fetus, or baby

READ MORE

Hibbert, Clare. *Terrible Tales of Ancient Greece.* Monstrous Myths. New York: Gareth Stevens Publishing, 2014.

Hoena, Blake. *The Voyages of Odysseus: A Graphic Retelling.* Ancient Myths. North Mankato, Minn.: Capstone Press, 2015.

Krieg, Katherine. *What We Get from Greek Mythology.* Mythology and Culture. Ann Arbor, Mich.: Cherry Lake Publishing, 2015.

Nardo, Don. *Odysseus.* A Kid's Guide to Mythology. Hockessin, Del.: Mitchell Lane Publishers, 2016.

INTERNET SITES

FactHound offers a safe, fun way to find Internet sites related to this book. All of the sites on FactHound have been researched by our staff.

Here's all you do:

Visit *www.facthound.com*

Type in this code: 9781515745846

Check out projects, games and lots more at
www.capstonekids.com

INDEX